RINGETTE RAVENS

Luca's First Try

STORY
by
HEATHER AND BEN THIESON

ART
by
TAYSON MARTINDALE

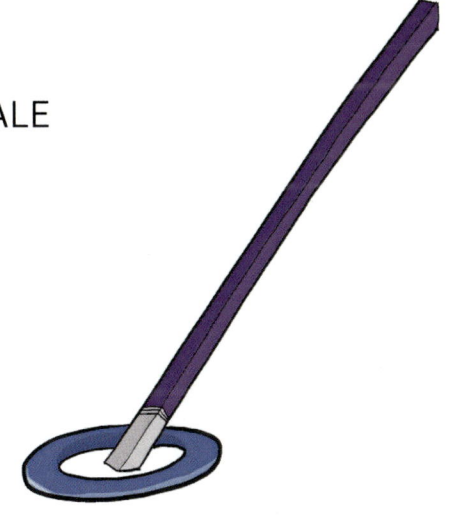

Special Thanks:

To our friends and family who read, edited, re-read, and edited again for us - Erik, Athena, Dee, Joel, Christina, Katie, and Mom & Dad. Thank you.

To our Illustrator, Tayson, who brought our words to life, and added so much charm and personality to our characters. Thank you for your creativity!

And to our daughters, Inara, and Luca, who somehow managed to keep this book a secret for the 2 years it took to create, and constantly helped us with capturing the voices of people much younger than we are.
Thank you!

This is a work of fiction. Short of naming 2 characters after our kids, the names, characters, events and incidents are the products of the author's imagination. Any resemblance to actual persons, living or dead, or actual events is purely coincidental.

Dedicated to every child
looking for their passion

"She's a firecracker!" I heard Dad say to Mom.

"Luca's got more energy than a kangaroo on a trampoline. She needs a sport, something to channel all that zip and zing into. We should find something just right for her."

And so my great sports adventure began. But wait- I'm getting ahead of myself.
Hi there, I'm Luca!

I'm eight years old, as cute as a button, strong as an ox, and Mom says I'm as stubborn as a mule!

And boy, I love to move -swing, jump, run, climb- you name it, that's me!

Mom always said when I found my 'thing', I'd be unstoppable. So, I had to try a whole bunch of 'things'.

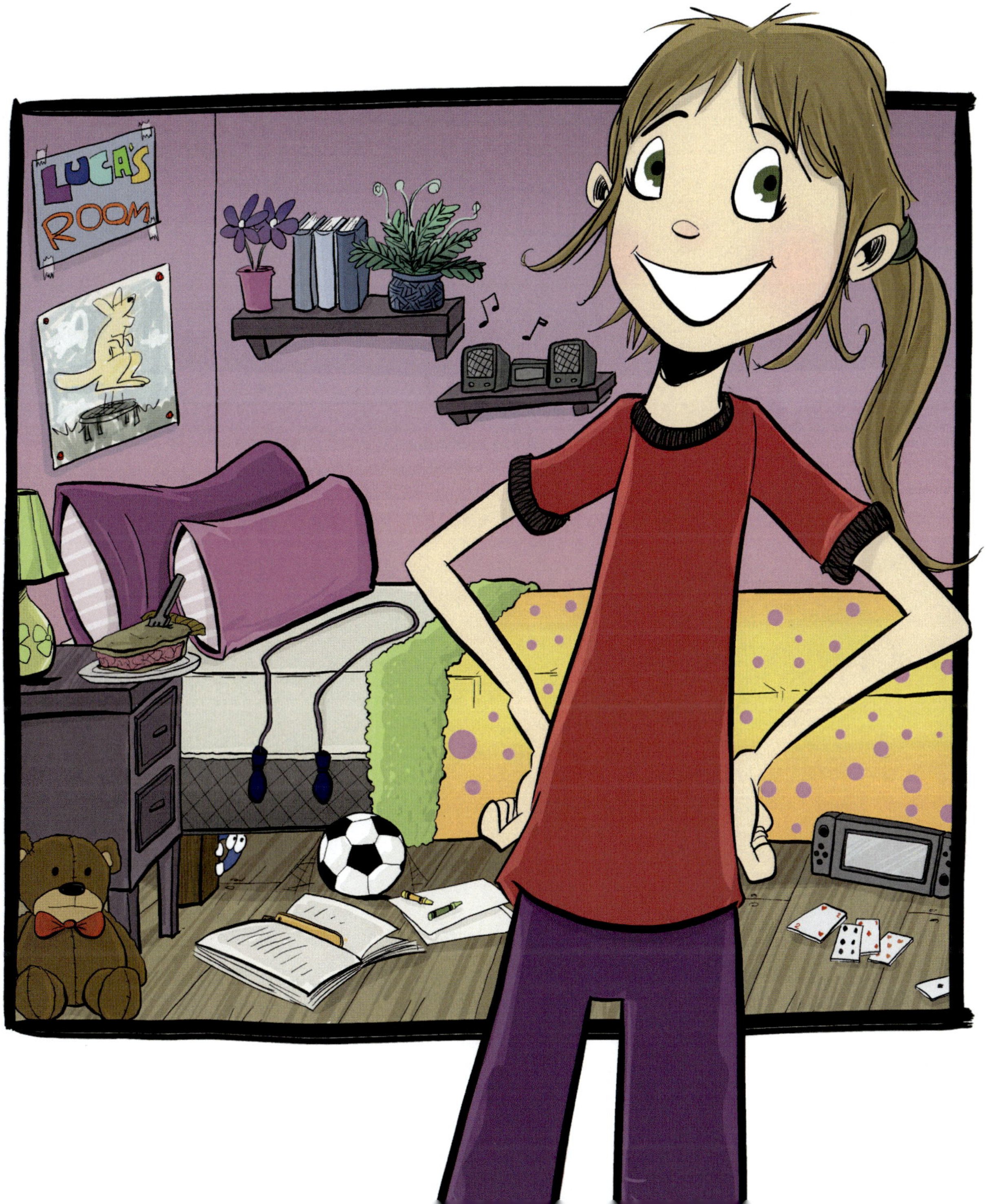
LUCA'S
ROOM

I jumped into gymnastics, but I was too short for the uneven bars

I tried soccer, but I hated when they gave us orange slices at half-time and my hands got all sticky!

I took a swing at baseball, but as it turns out, I don't like people throwing balls at my head.

I dove into swimming, but the pool water made me itch all over.

Then one day, my Mom brought up ringette.

In my mind, I saw a sprawling green field, towering pylons, and giant hula hoops being flung towards them. She had my attention!

"Well," Mom began, "it's a bit like ice hockey, but you swap out a curved stick for a straight one, and change out the puck for a ring. Plus, it's much faster." Then she played a clip of a ringette game, and it was so quick it made my head spin! Once the video ended, she turned to me and asked, "so, what do you think? Would you like to give it a shot?"

"No way, not for me," I replied instantly. But Mom and Dad have this rule - I have to try something at least once before I can decide I don't like it. So, without missing a beat, Mom signed me up for a trial class that Saturday. She promised that if I didn't enjoy it, I wouldn't have to continue. So I guess I was going to try ringette.

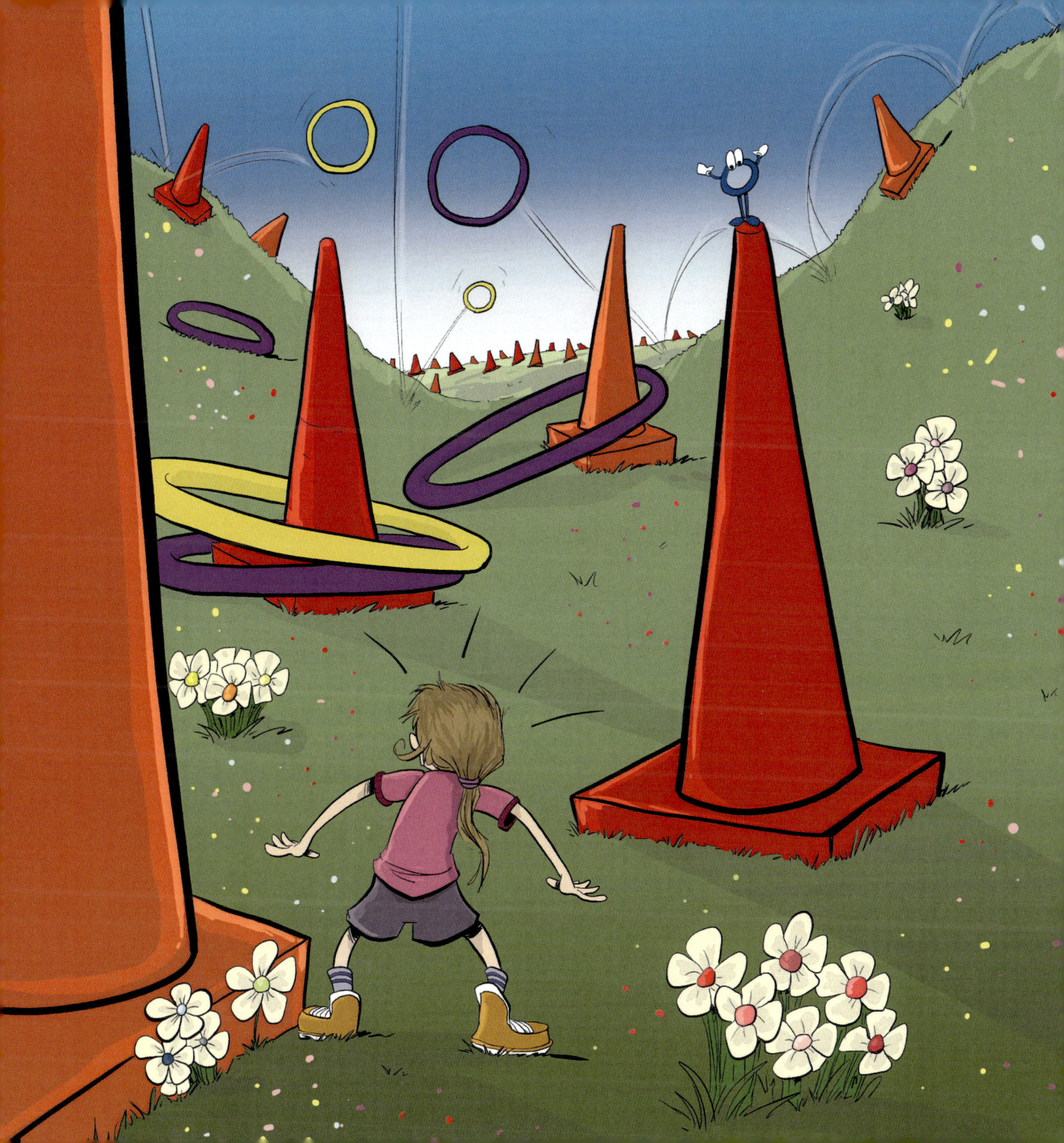

My tummy was doing somersaults! I had wrangled up some pads and gear from friends, but my skates had been gathering dust for a whole year. "What if I'm no good at this?" I was stressed and nervous, but I had pinky-promised Mom and Dad that I'd give it a shot and I wasn't about to back down now.

When I got to the ice rink, I even got to borrow a practice jersey from another family and I transformed into an actual ringette player! I was decked out from head to toe, and let me tell you, I felt like a million bucks. I couldn't help but strut around a little. It was really fun to imagine I was an actual player, getting ready for the big game!

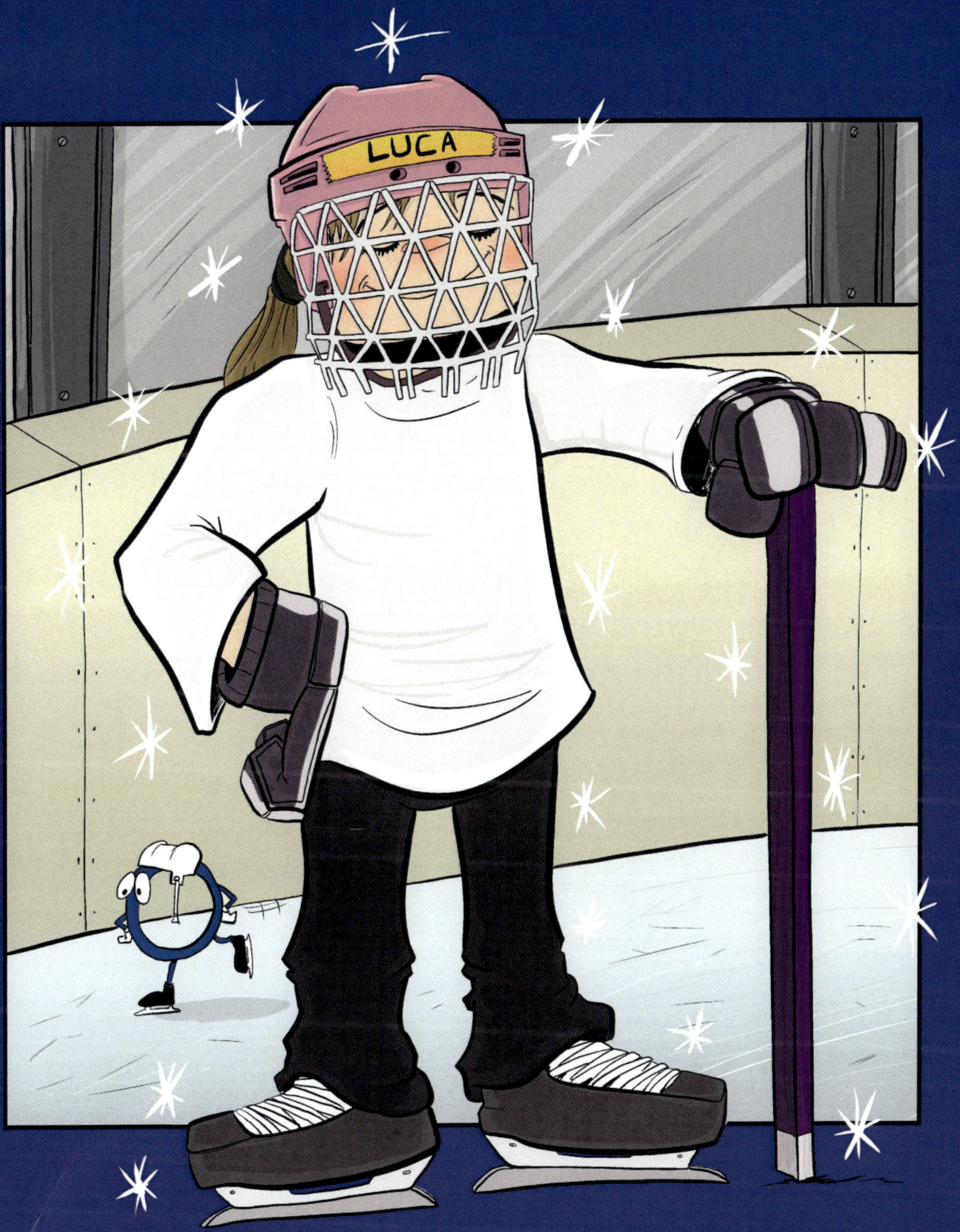
LUCA

On the ice, oh boy my legs were wobbly! The coaches made us laugh and taught us games, and then we started with basics, and ringette drills.

We learned how the ice is divided in sections, marked by blue lines. In ringette you can't bring the ring across a blue line with you - you need to pass it to a teammate to get it across. Then we got to try it out. I felt like a new baby giraffe standing there in my skates. I was trying to pass the ring, and not fall down in the process, but it seemed to slip and slide everywhere except where it was supposed to go!

Even though I was struggling, everyone cheered and encouraged me. I had a feeling ringette was going to be fun.

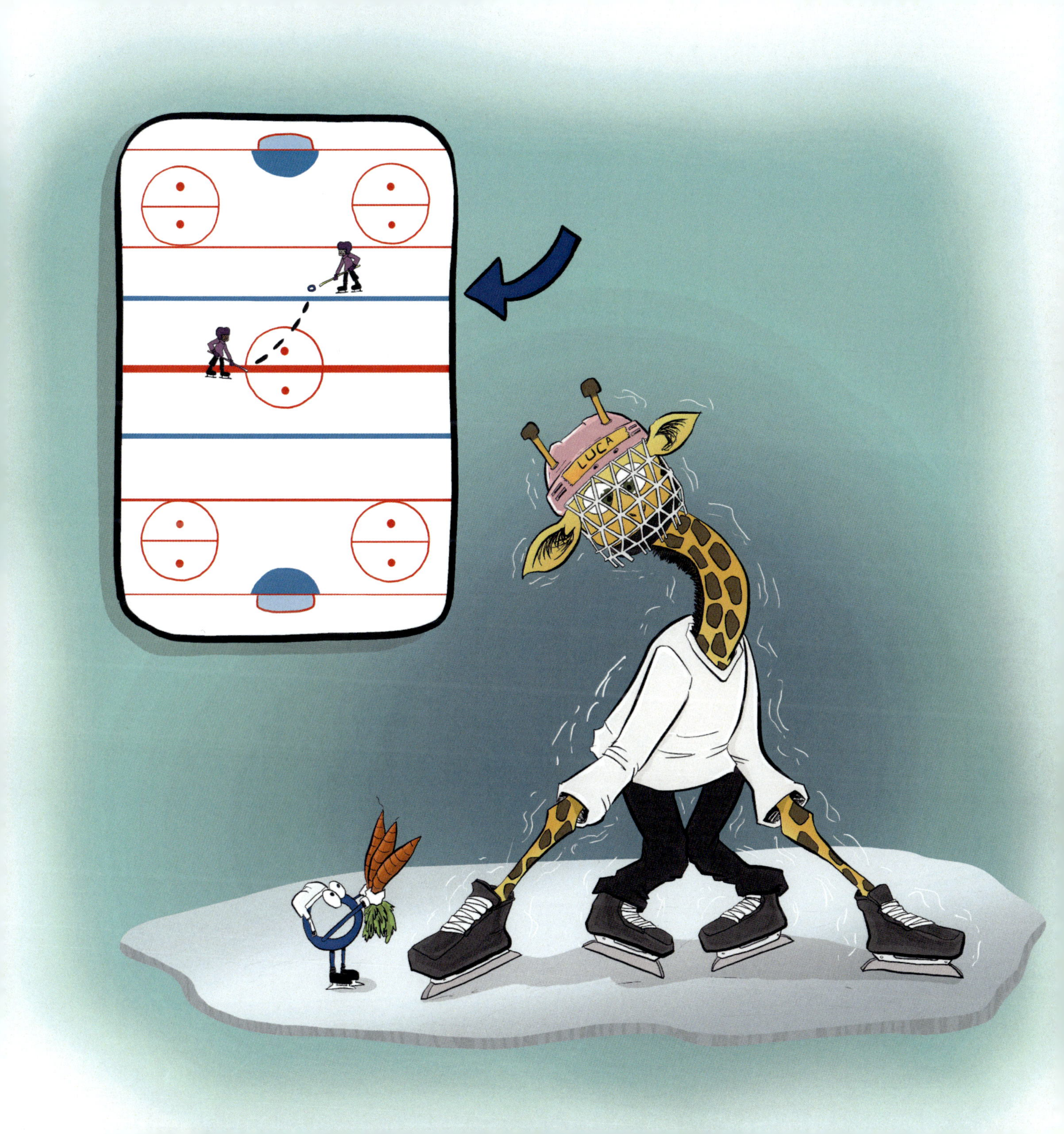
LUCA

When I got off the ice, mom was waiting for me in the locker room. I couldn't stop smiling, as I told her "Sign me up!" This was it, I had finally found my sport. I was going to be Luca the Ringette Player! I could just see it now. One day everyone in the stands will be cheering my name. Now I just had to figure out how I was going to get through the next few weeks until the season started.

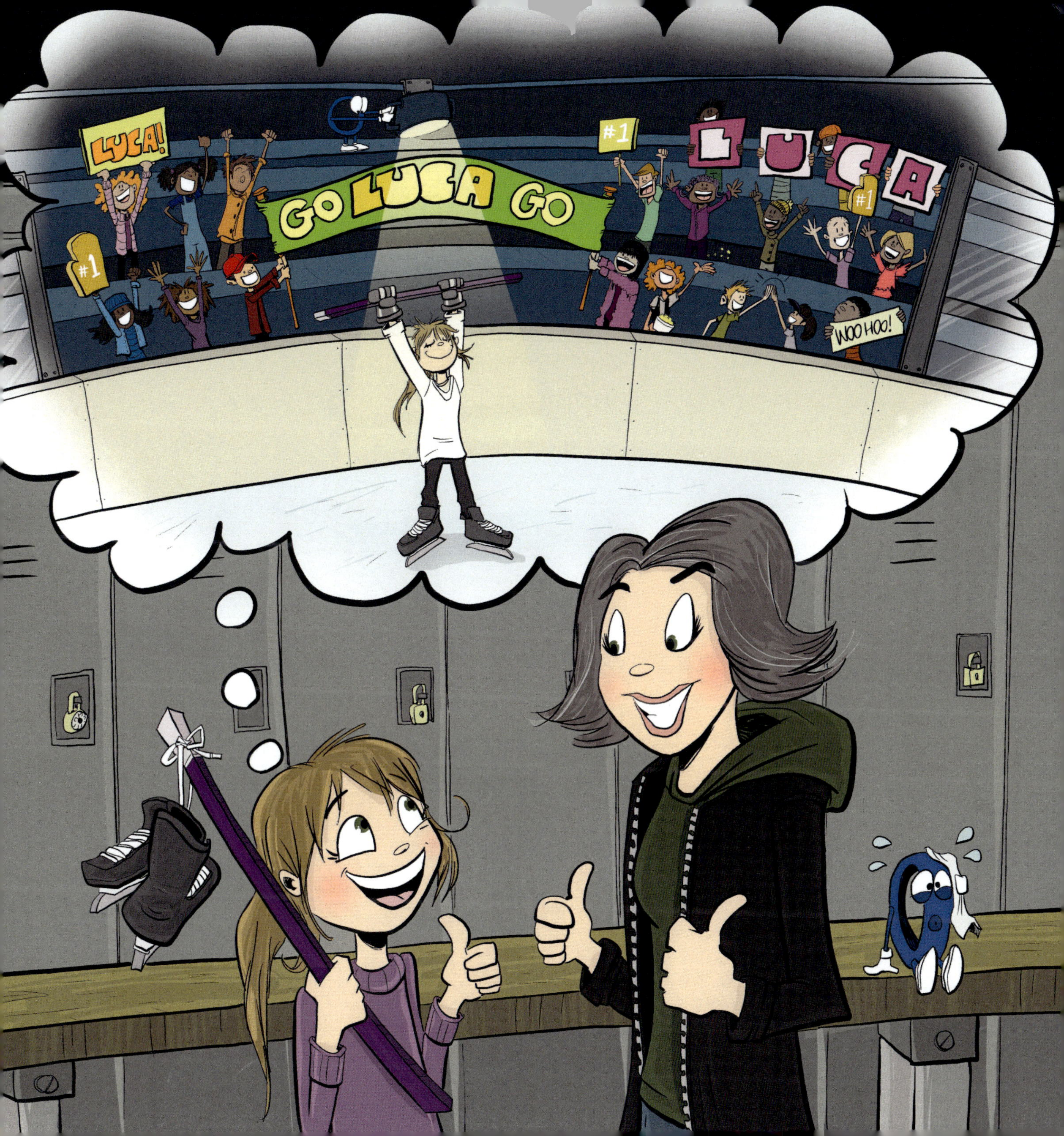
LUCA!
#1
GO LUCA GO
#1
L U C A
#1
#1
WOO HOO!

It was the day of the big game; I was wearing my jersey - the mighty #22 - and I was ready. When my skates connected with the ice, and I pushed myself over the smooth hard surface, it felt like I was weightless.

We got into position, the screech of the whistle went and immediately I flew across the blue line, snagged a great pass from my teammate, and took off!

I was as fast as lightning as I streaked toward the goal with my stick pinning the ring to the ice. The other team was coming after me, but they couldn't catch me. I was a powerful freight train going full speed ahead and nothing could stop me!

I approached the net with a look of determination on my face. This was it, this was my moment, all eyes were on me as the crowd went silent. I flipped the ring up to the tip of my stick in one smooth motion and sent it sailing into the back of the net before the goalie even knew what had happened!

BEEP! BEEP! BEEP! BEEP!

Immediately the crowd erupted in cheers. "Luca! Luca! Luca!" My team surrounded me and lifted me high off my skates into the air! My coach skated over to me, beaming like the sun, but when she opened her mouth, all she said was "Beep Beep Beep Bee…."

Poof! The ice, the cheers and the glory, all vanished into thin air. There I was, not on a frosty rink, but snuggled in my cozy bed. The beeping? It wasn't my coach, it was my pesky alarm clock yapping that it was time to get up for school. My heart sank a little as I realized it had all been a dream.

I grumbled like a bear waking from hibernation and reached over to silence the beeping. With dreams of ringette still dancing in my head, I hopped out of bed and got dressed for another day of school

The very next day, at my first-ever ringette practice, I imagined myself as graceful as a figure skater. But, oh dear, reality had a different plan! Dressed in new gear that made me look like a pro, I felt like I could conquer the world. But as soon as my skates hit the ice, I turned into a wobbly duckling. My skates and I weren't the best of friends yet, and they seemed to have a mind of their own.

My coach's name was Lisa, and I liked her immediately. Her smile could have powered the entire city. She was like a burst of sunshine on a cloudy day. Coach Lisa was cheerful and so encouraging, you just couldn't help but smile when she talked to you.

Coach Lisa was a Ringette Master! She zipped around the ice with the grace of an ice fairy and had an endless bag of tips and tricks that she sprinkled on us like magic dust. Coach Lisa also showed us how to grip our sticks just right, how to glide with the ring, and even how to pat each other on the top of the helmet as a way of saying "Good job!"

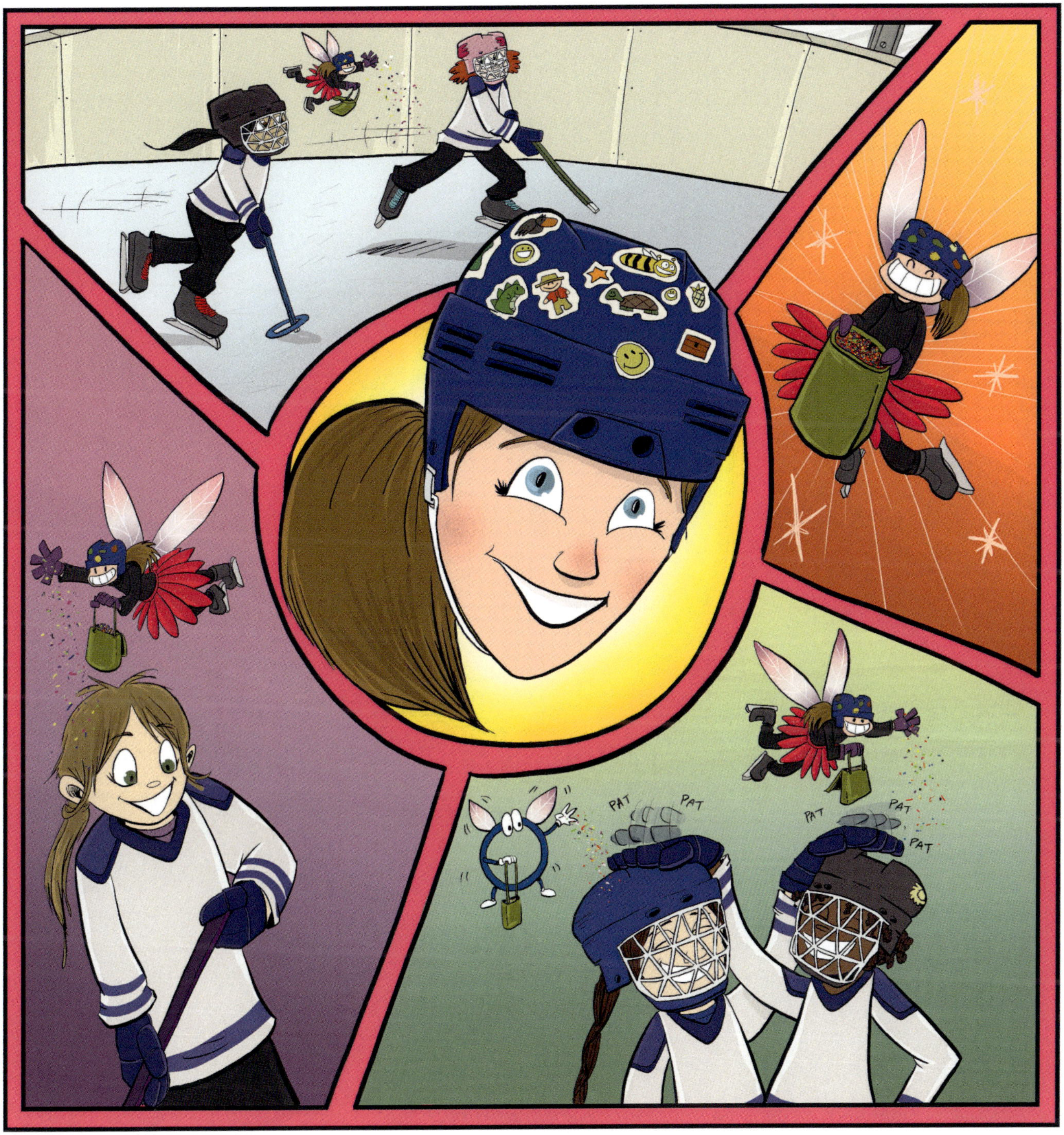
PAT
PAT
PAT
PAT
PAT

We ended up having 11 girls on our team. One was the girl I sat beside in the change room during the trial class. Her name was Stella and she was so happy we were playing together. Stella's older sister had played the year before, but this was her first year, just like me.

Coach Lisa taught us that a team is like a family, and families know and trust each other. So, she gathered us in a circle on the ice and said, "Let's get to know our ringette family!"

First up was little ol' me! I practically yelled, "I love to dance and move almost as much as I love gobbling chocolate ice cream! And guess what? I've got a dog AND a black cat!"

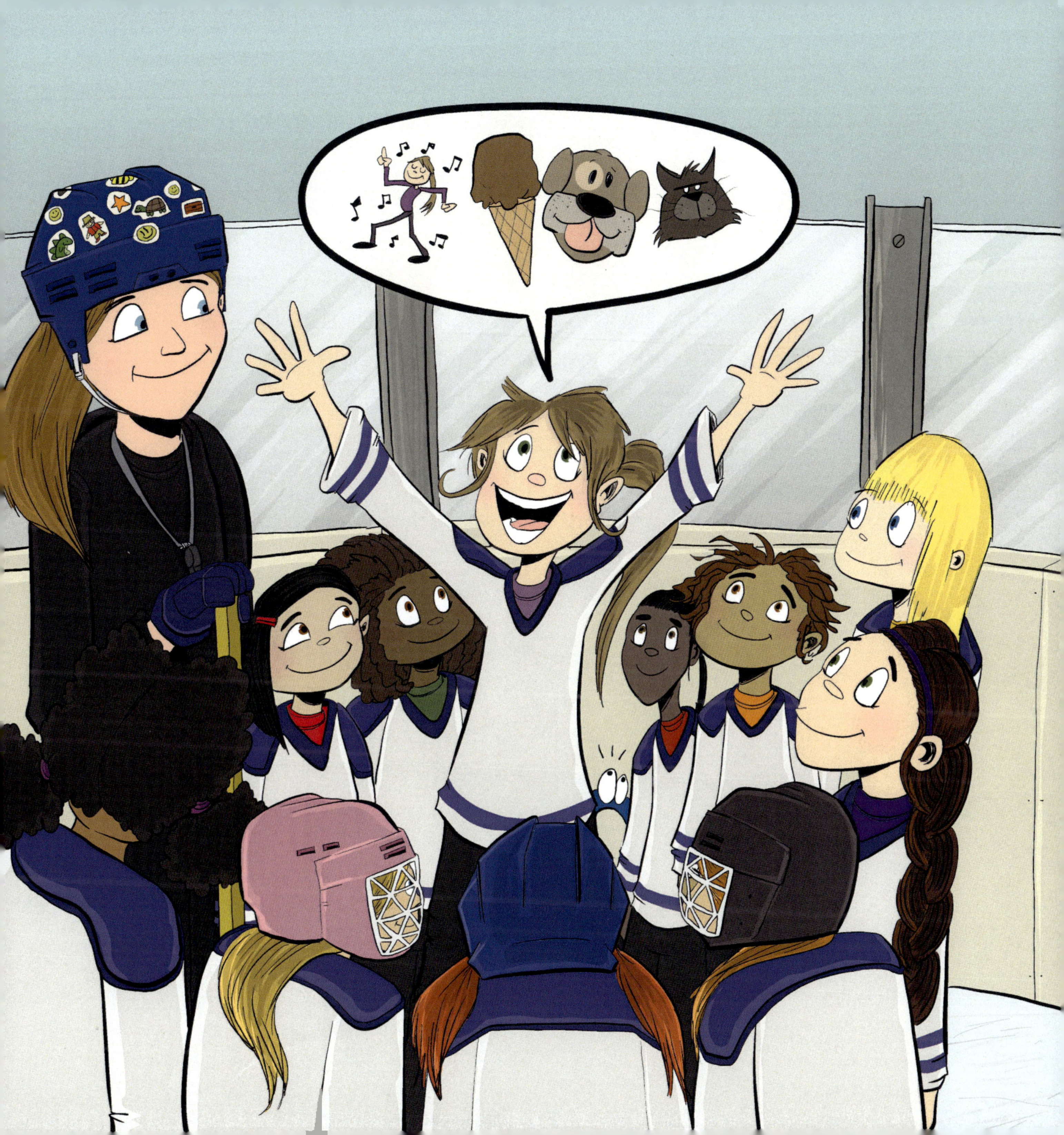

One by one the girls took turns introducing themselves.

Inara had dark hair so long and thick it could have been Rapunzel's. It was braided all the way down to her bum. She declared, "I adore books, I REALLY want to play goalie and I also have a chubby black cat who thinks he's a king!" We both grinned at each other – cat twins!

Next was Gabby. She had curls springing out from under her helmet that reminded me of flowers. She told us all about her singing lessons, and then added "Also, my dad's enchiladas are the BEST, and I'll bring them to practice!" My tummy rumbled - I couldn't wait for that day.

Then there was Ripley, with her bright blue eyes and white blond hair. She zoomed around on one foot and said, "I've been skating since I was three and I can do 20 cartwheels in a row." I thought, "Cartwheel challenge, here we come!"

And of course, Stella, my buddy! She told us she was the youngest of three kids in her family and spent a whole year in the stands watching her sister play just waiting for her turn. Her eyes sparkled as she added, "I can't wait to play ringette with all of you."

I really liked being on the ice, but it was a little like stepping into a world where the ground could slip away at any moment, and I would come crashing down face first. My legs were still jelly, so I decided to take it nice and slow. I was starting to get the hang of pushing off with my skates to glide, saying the words as I went.

"Push….glide…. push….glide….push….glide".

I felt like I was picking up speed when I suddenly realized something terrible - I didn't know how to stop yet! And I was headed straight for Stella!

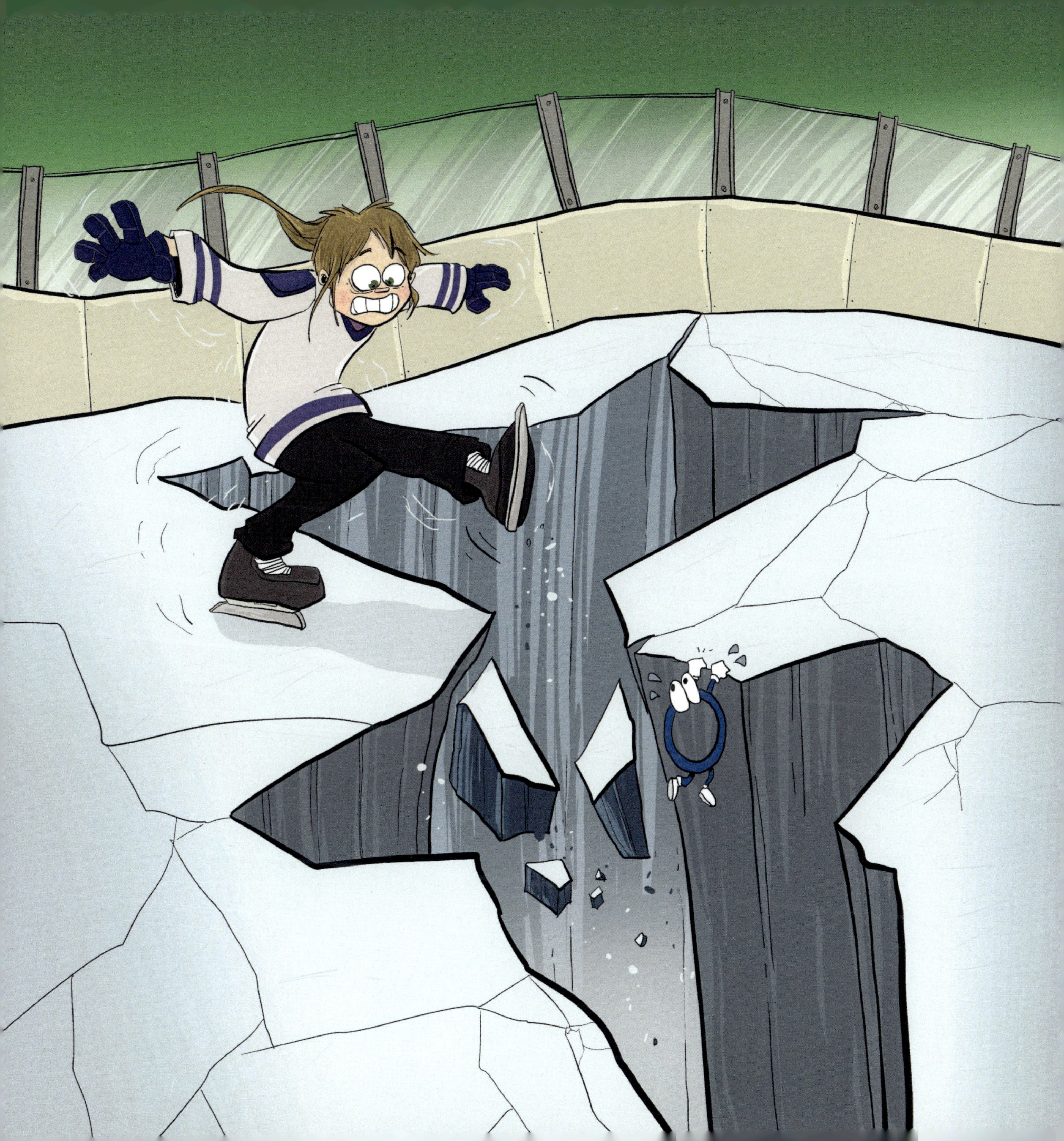

Stella and I collided with a bang and we both toppled backwards onto the ice. I tensed up, preparing for the pain. But guess what? No pain came! I was okay! I quickly checked on Stella, and to my surprise, she was laughing. She was okay too. My helmet and all those pads and guards I had strapped to my body had protected me. I didn't have to be scared of falling anymore. In fact, falling was actually kind of fun. I was going to be OKAY!

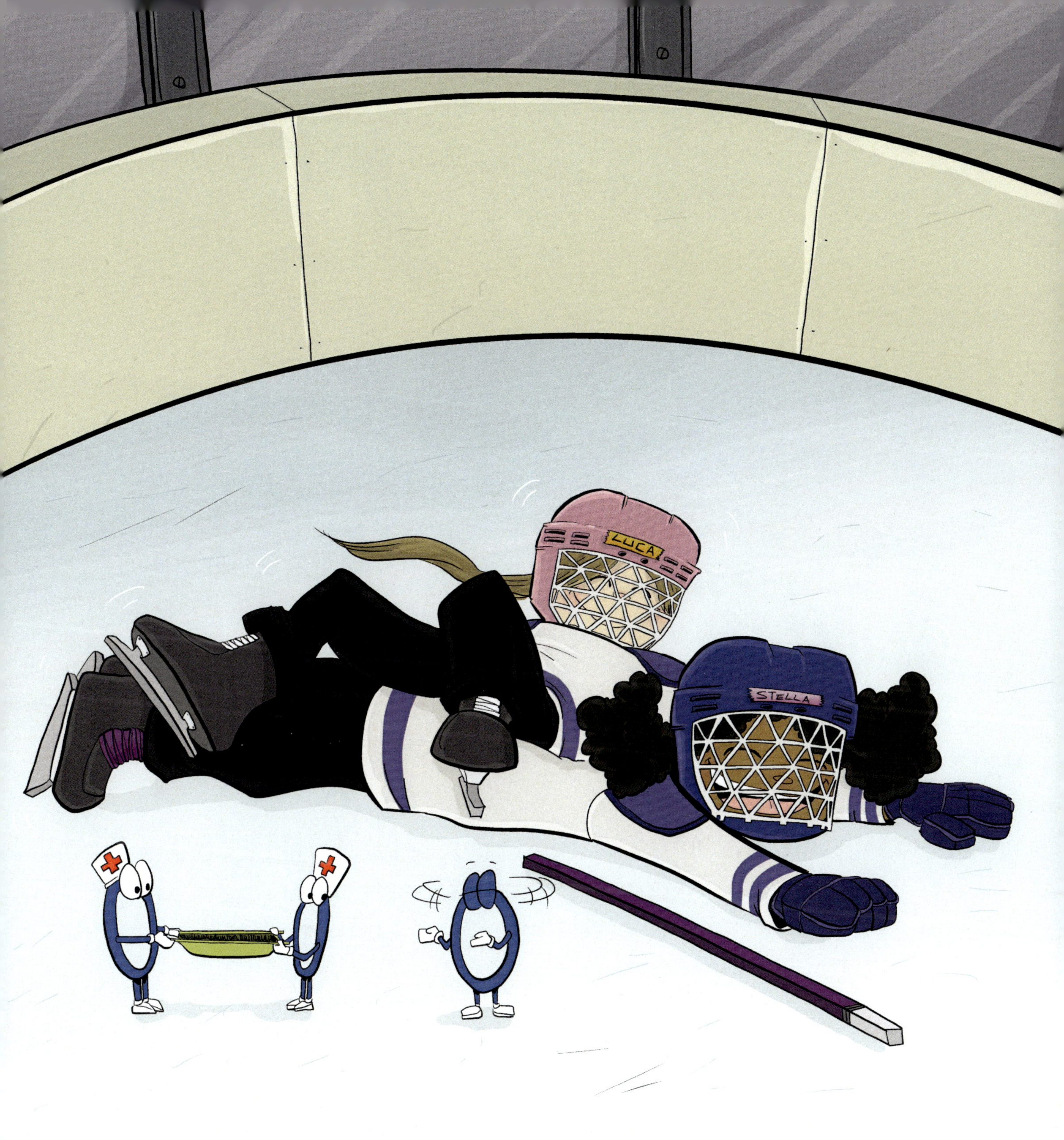
LUCA
STELLA

In an instant my jersey seemed to dissolve and in its place emerged a suit of gleaming armor, transforming me into an invincible warrior on ice. Nothing could harm me now. I was untouchable!

With this newfound armour, I charged ahead, pushing myself to skate faster than I had ever dared before.

After practice, Coach Lisa had a cool surprise for us. She showed us our new team jerseys and said we could pick our favourite number to wear for the season. Immediately Inara's hand shot straight up as she blurted out "Which one is the goalie jersey?" I laughed. Inara was always talking about being a goalie.

My eyes scanned the jerseys hanging on the wall and then I saw it, number 22. I remembered my dream, it felt like it was meant to be. I picked up number 22 and tried it on. It fit just right. I was so happy, I couldn't stop smiling!

Coach Lisa caught my grin and shouted "Lu 22! That's awesome!" Somehow my smile got even bigger, now I had a new jersey and a nickname!

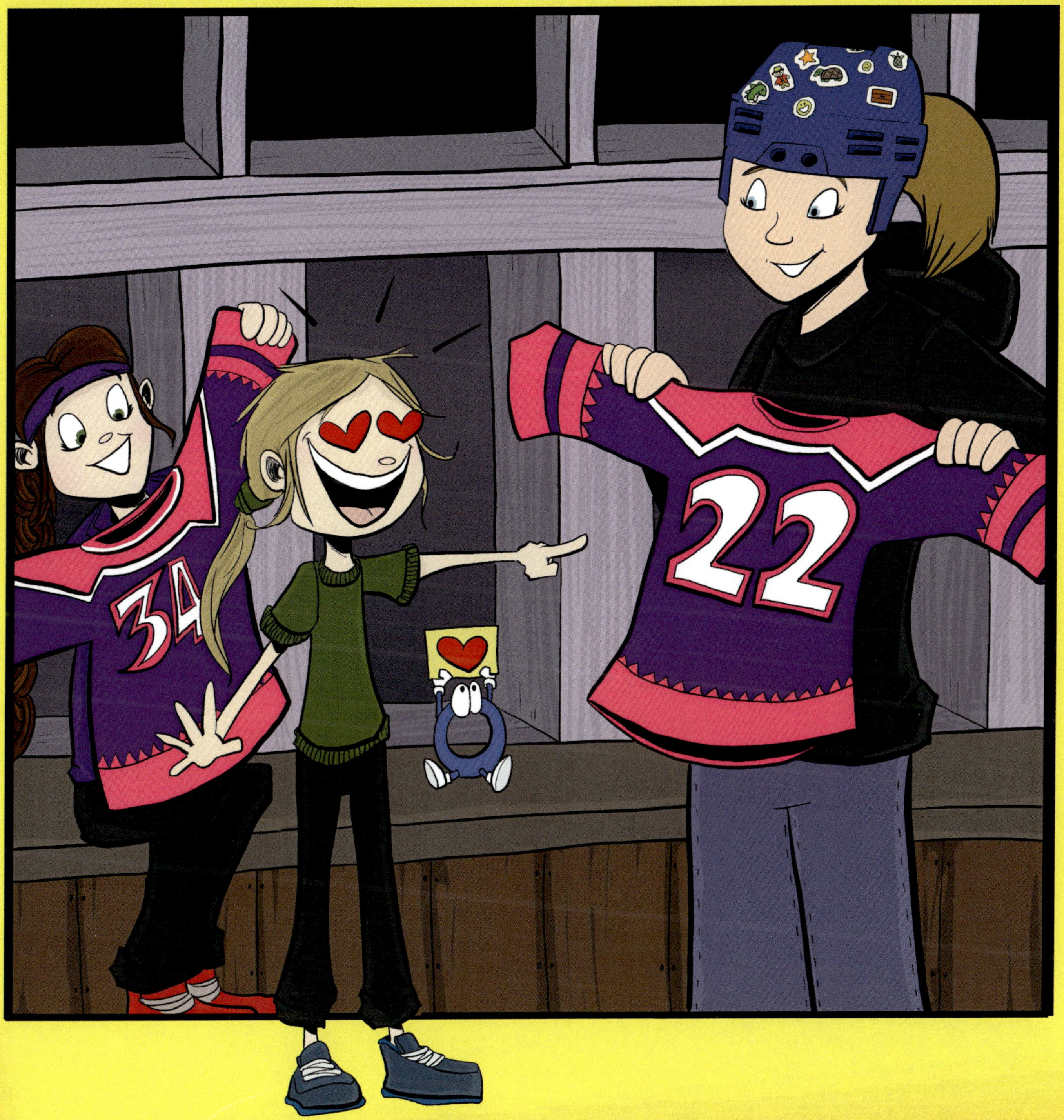
34
22

Coach Lisa had another surprise up her sleeve. She let us choose our own team name! Excitement filled the air as everyone on the team huddled together, brainstorming and giggling.

Each player weighed in and we took turns suggesting different names. After much discussion and laughter, we finally cast our votes and became the Ravens!

It was a perfect fit. From that moment on, we were the Ravens, ready to take flight!

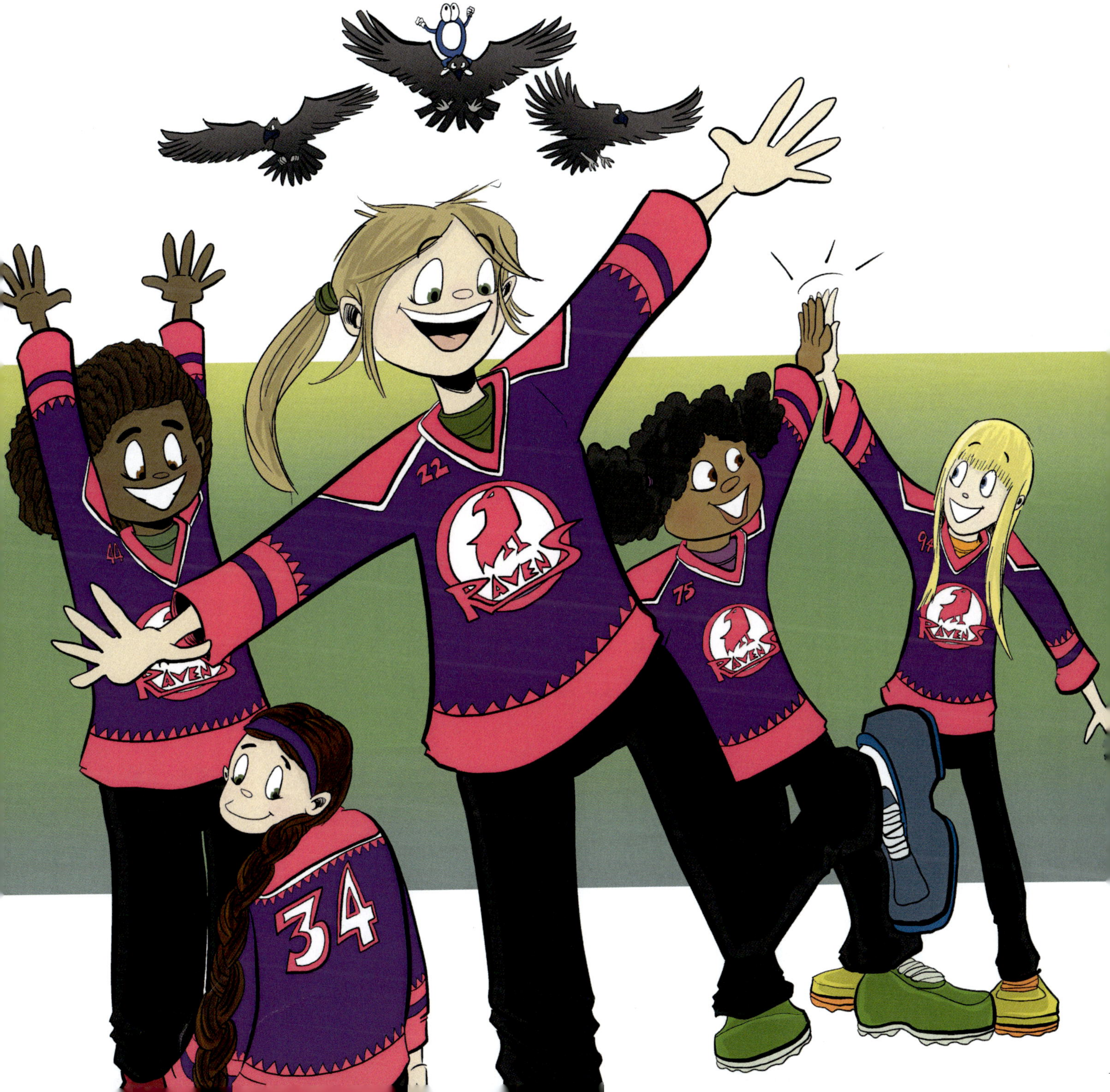
22
RAVENS
75
34

On the morning of our first game I was super excited and nervous all at once. Dad noticed I looked a bit worried when he was tying my skates. "What's up, Luca?" he asked.

"Dad, what if I trip or fall or make a mistake? What if I forget to pass at the blue line or something?"

Dad gave me a big smile, "You probably will at first, everyone makes mistakes, Lu. Especially when they are just learning. If you fall or you forget, just try again and don't forget to have fun!"

Stella, who was next to me, giggled, "Remember when we both fell during practice? It was so funny!" We both laughed, thinking about our big crash.

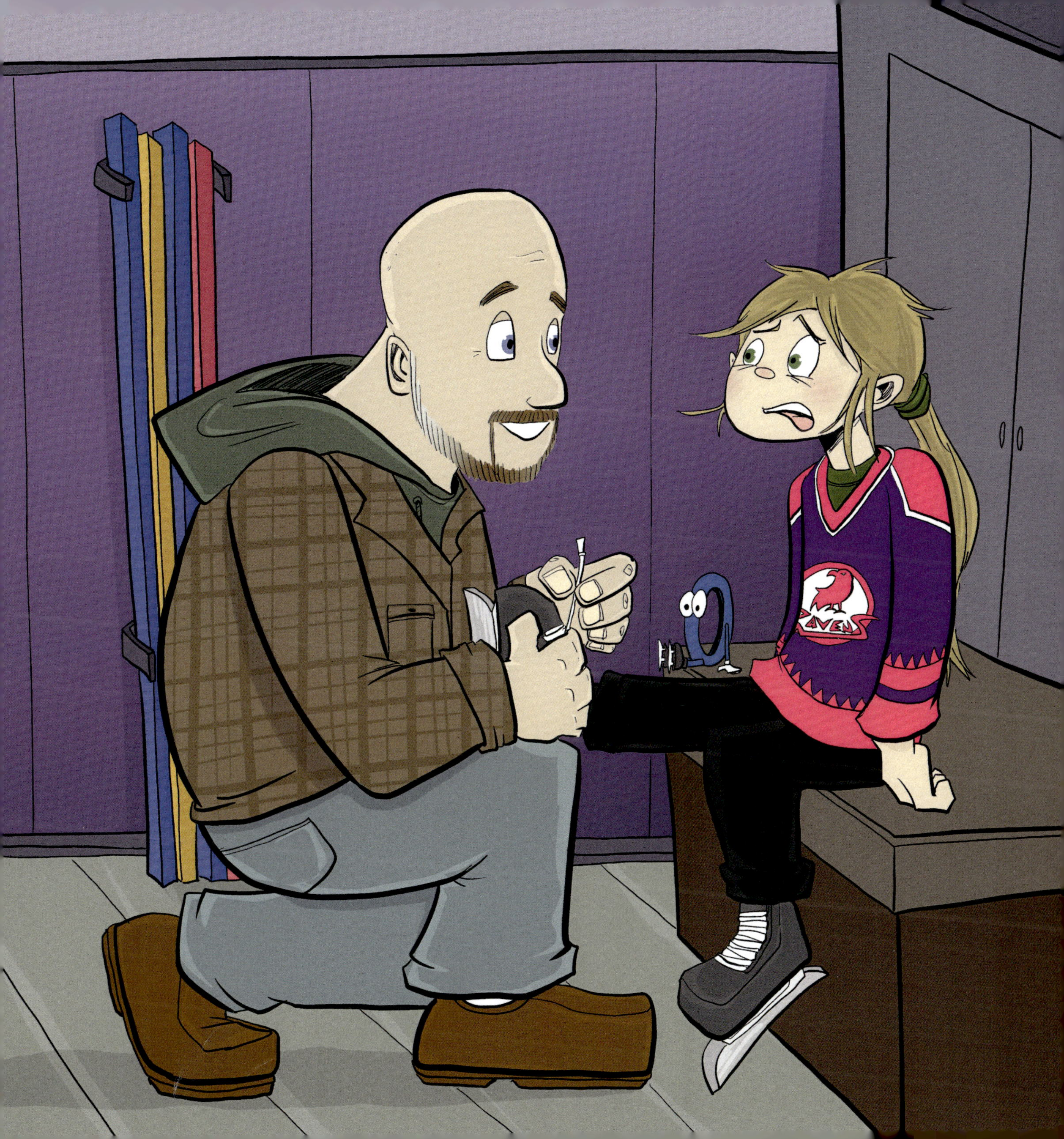
Ravens

Coach Lisa gathered us in a huddle, but before she could speak, Inara's voice piped up, "Coach Lisa, can I be the goalie today?"

Coach Lisa smiled at all of us and then said "Today is about doing your best, working hard, and having fun! And yes, Inara, you can be our goalie for this game!"
Inara's face lit up, "Thank you Coach, I'll do my best!"

"Before we get on the ice we need to figure out a team cheer" said Coach Lisa.

"Let's caw like Ravens!" yelled Ripley.
So we left the locker room waving our arms up and down and loudly shouting "CAW CAW CAW!"

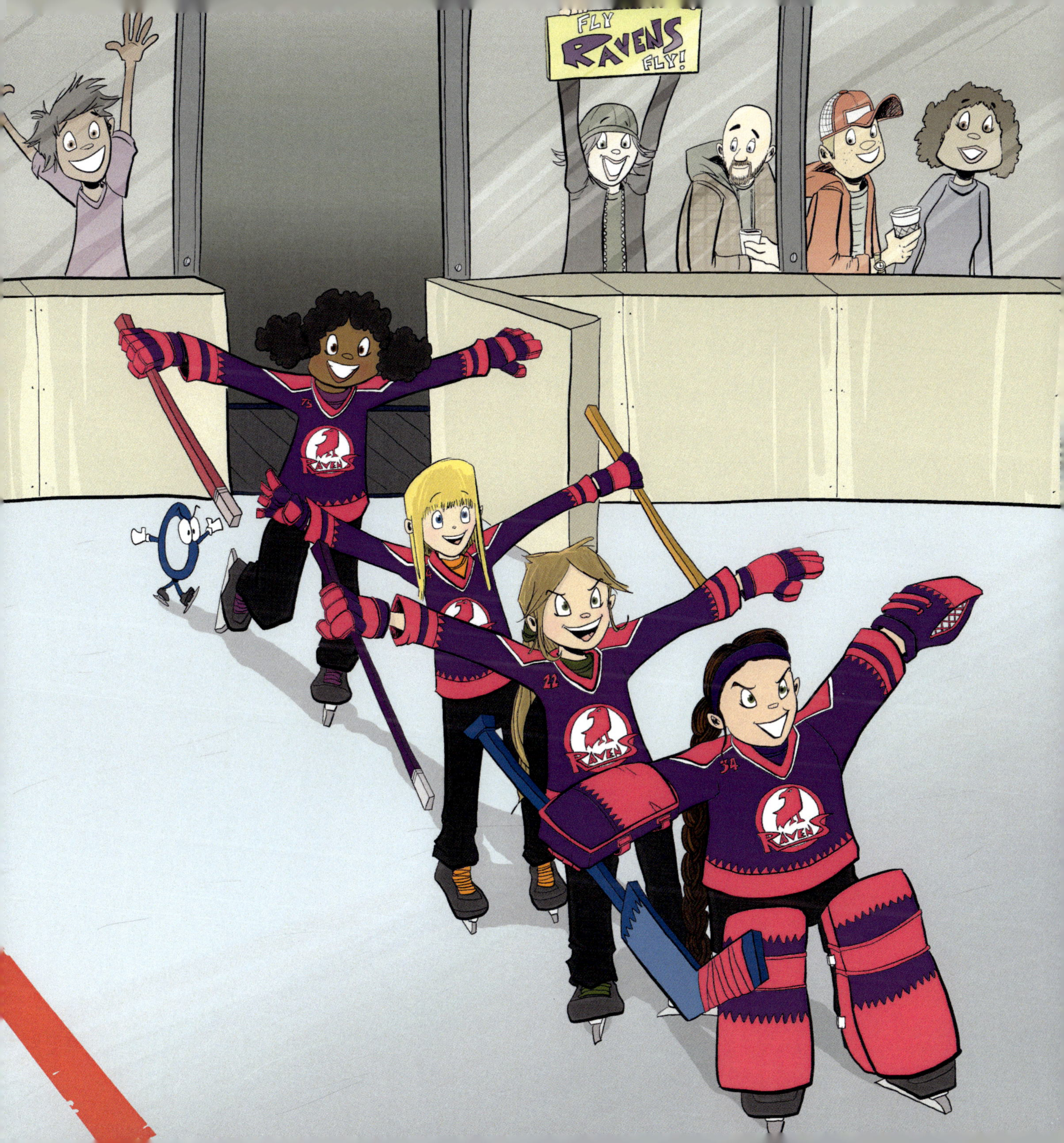
FLY RAVENS FLY!

As I stepped onto the ice, the cool air brushed against my face sending a shiver of excitement down my spine. The rink was alive with the sound of skates scraping the ice and the chatter of players warming up. I started with some basic drills, gliding from one side of the boards to the other, practicing my stops and starts.

As I was doing a figure-eight, I noticed a player from the opposing team skating towards me. She had a bright red jersey with the number 7 on the back and a head of curly brown hair peeking out from under her helmet.

"Hi!" she called out, skating up to me. "I'm Charlie."
"Hi, Charlie! I'm Luca," I replied.

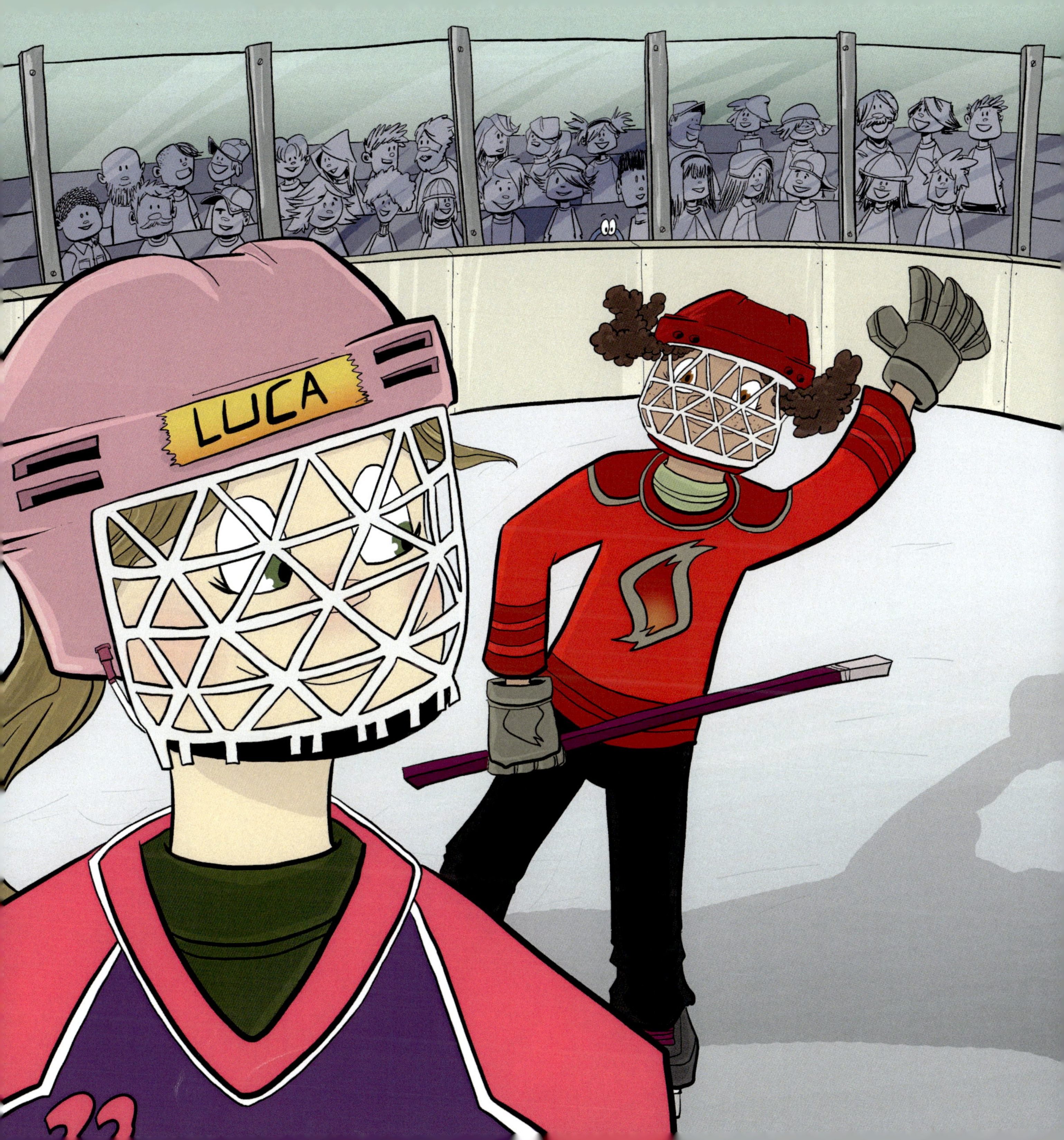
LUCA

Charlie's smile was wide, and showed she was missing a tooth right in the front. "Are you excited for the game?" she asked.

I grinned, "I am, but I'm also little nervous, it's my first game and I'm still getting the hang of things."

Charlie laughed, "Don't worry, you'll do great. It's really fun and I never even know what the score is during games anyway."

I always thought team sports meant that there would be this battle against other players, but ringette just felt different. Charlie's words just made me even more excited for the match ahead.

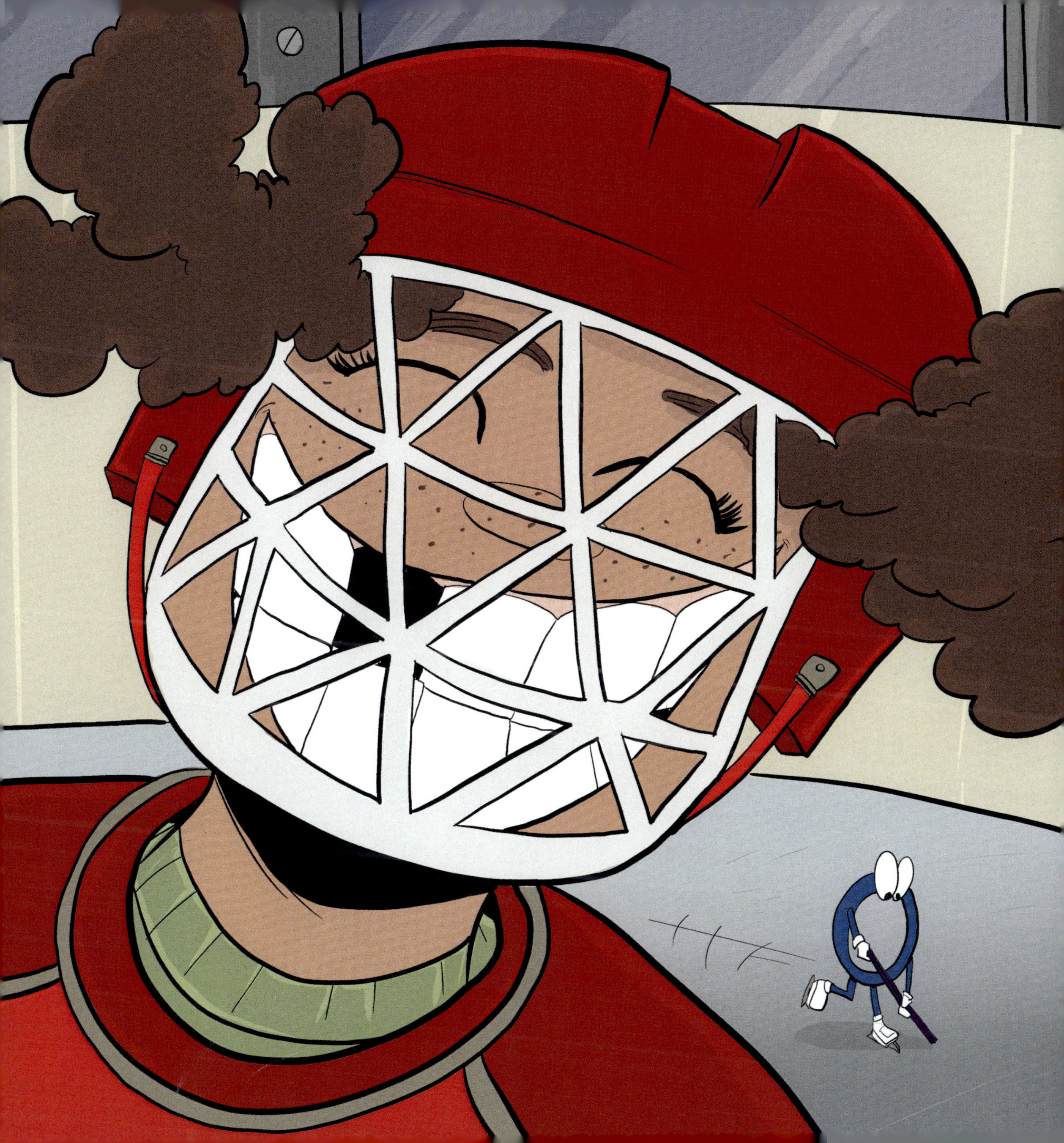

Once the game began, it was very clear that the other team had had more practice than we did. It was like a terrible game of keep-away, where we never got the ring. I finally managed to stab the ring with my stick and passed it to Gabby.

She paused for a moment as she tried to figure out her next move, but it was long enough for the other team to swoop in and take the ring back, like a team of professional ring robbers.

Ripley tried to intercept the pass between the other team over the blue line, but turned too quickly and lost her balance.

Thankfully, Inara made up for our mistakes by saving shot after shot! I was so happy Coach let her play goalie!

As the game went on, we started to click like puzzle pieces finding their matching partners. "Over to Stella!", "Pass to me, I'm open!" We really started talking to each other. As we played, every shout, and pass made us work more like a complete machine.

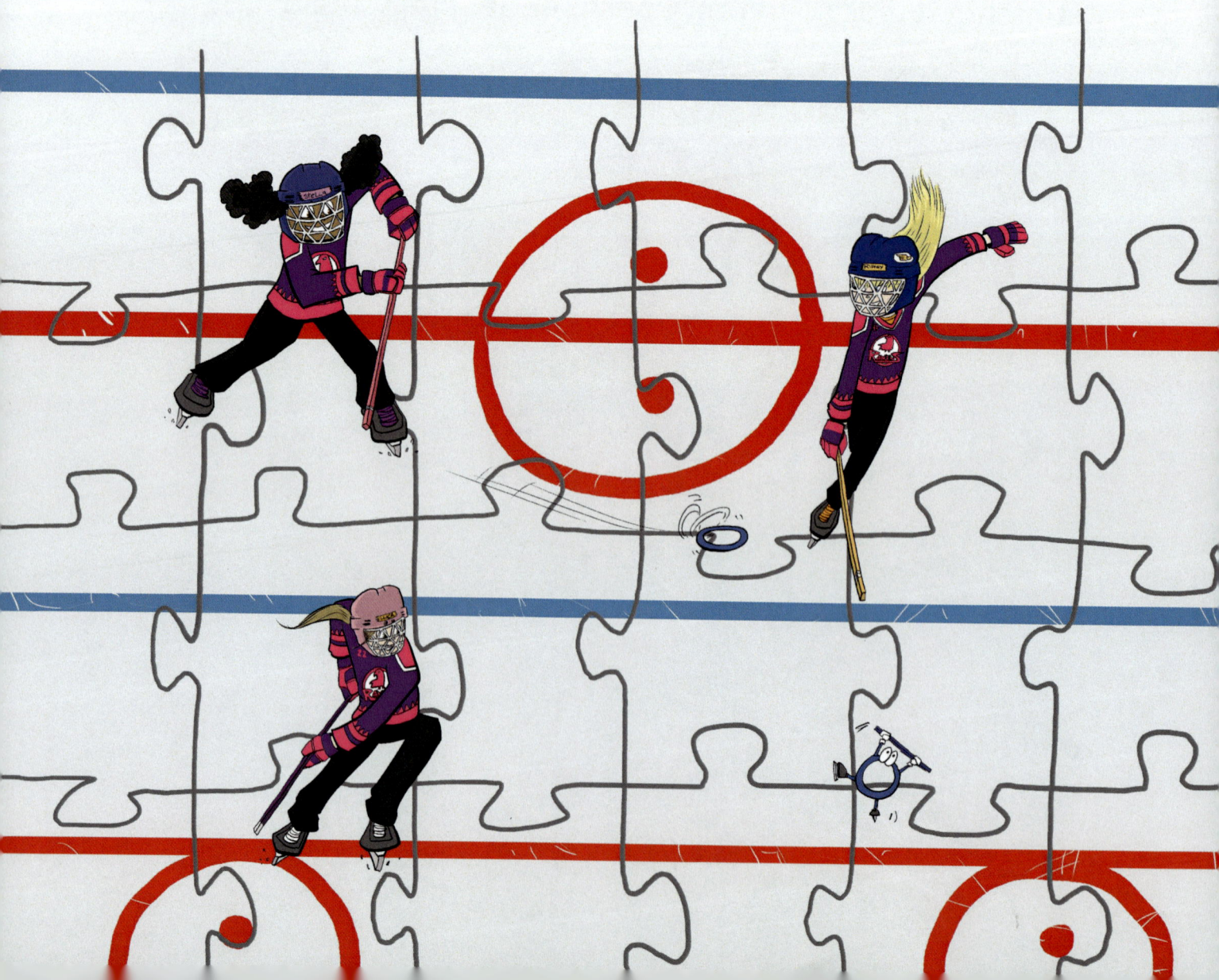

Gabby and Ripley teamed up to deliver the ring to Stella and she sent it sailing into the net. When we got to halftime, thanks to Inara stopping almost all of the shots sent to her and our newfound teamwork, we were finally feeling like we might have a chance in this game.

The second half of the game started and we had found our rhythm. Stella passed the ring to me over the blue line and an opening appeared. My heart raced as I zoomed towards the goal, the crowd's cheers becoming a distant roar. Just as I was about to make my move, my skates betrayed me, sending me sprawling onto the ice as graceful as a rhino on rollerblades

The fall happened in slow motion. I was falling through jelly, but on my way down I managed to shove my stick forward with the ring still on it.

As I lay there, momentarily dazed, the arena fell silent. I couldn't see where the ring had landed. Did I miss the net? Was my first shot a dud?

But then, a sudden burst of cheers shattered the silence. I looked up to see Stella and my new friend Charlie, from the other team, both beaming down at me. I turned to look at the net and my heart soared. The ring was in. It was a goal!

Charlie extended a hand to help me up. "That was awesome!" she exclaimed, grinning ear to ear.

Stella was by my side a second later patting the top of my helmet. "You got your first goal!" Stella cheered!

"I couldn't have done it without that amazing pass!" I said, turning to Stella and patting the top of her helmet with a grin.

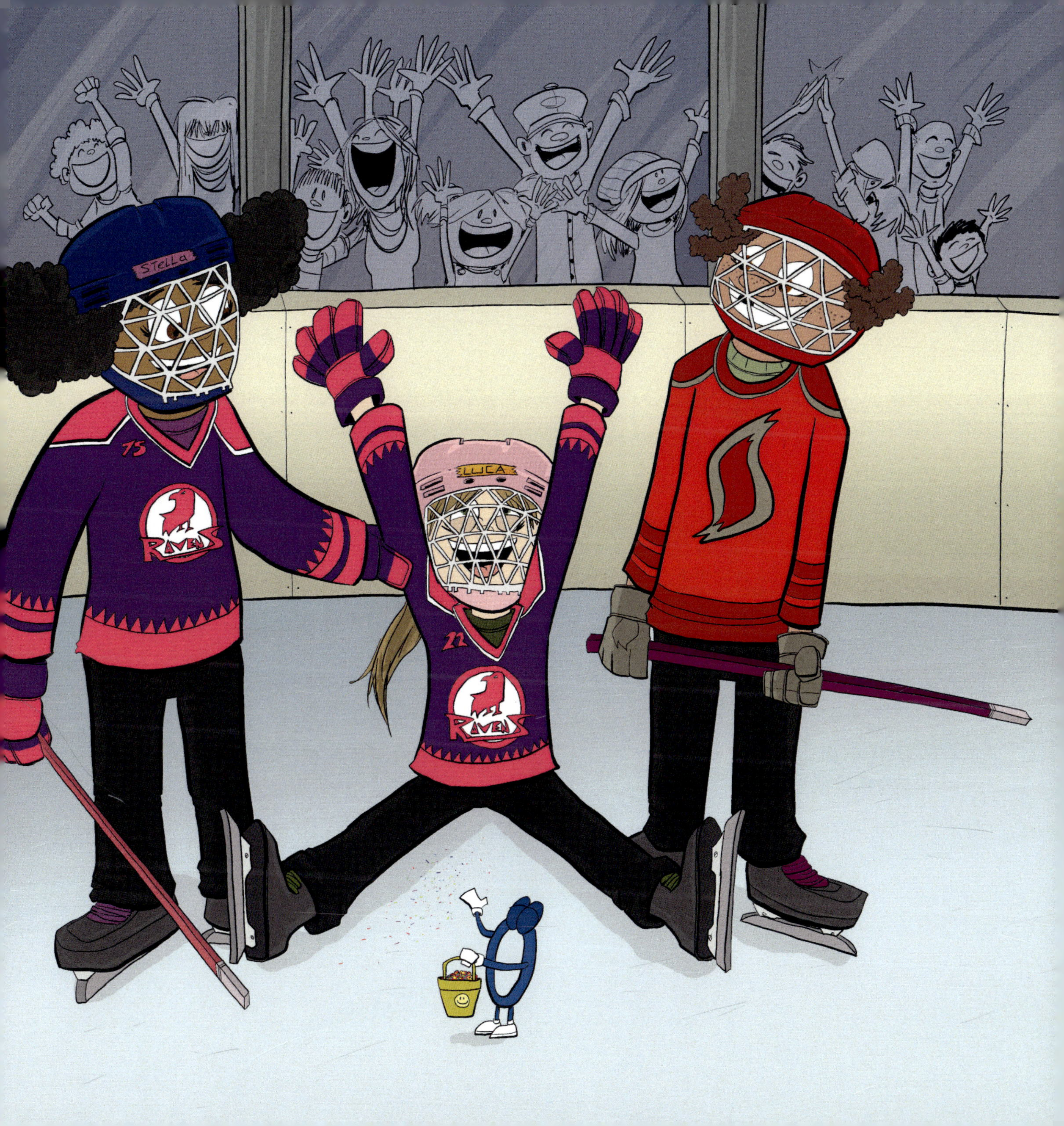
STELLA
LUCA
75
RAVENS
22
RAVENS

Later on, as we left the rink, Mom and Dad couldn't stop gushing over how proud of me they were, and it felt really good. I realized I was really proud of myself too - and that felt even better.

My smile was so big, my cheeks were starting to hurt. Charlie was right too. I didn't even know what the score was or if we even won, and I didn't care! I just got my skates off and I couldn't wait to get them back on.

"Mom, Dad. Thanks for making me try ringette. I say we celebrate with milkshakes" I said. "I think that sounds like a great idea." said Mom.

I found my sport, but I found so much more. I'm not just Luca the Ringette Player. I'm a RAVEN!